Raccoon Family Adventures

Bobbie Kalman

Crabtree Publishing Company

www.crabtreebooks.com

Animal Family ADVENTURES

Created by Bobbie Kalman

For Clement Duquesne
Your mother met some raccoons at our home
when she was a child. Did she tell you the story?
Love, Bobbie, Peter, and Samantha

Author
Bobbie Kalman

Photo research
Bobbie Kalman

Editors
Kathy Middleton
Crystal Sikkens

Design
Bobbie Kalman
Katherine Berti

Print and production coordinator
Katherine Berti

Illustrations
Barbara Bedell: pages 4, 20 (top)

Photographs
Photodisc: page 20 (bottom)
Superstock: Fotosearch: page 5
Thinkstock: pages 13 (top), 14 (top right), 24,
    27 (bottom left)
Other images by Shutterstock

Library and Archives Canada Cataloguing in Publication

Kalman, Bobbie, author
        Raccoon family adventures / Bobbie Kalman.

(Animal family adventures)
Includes index.
Issued in print and electronic formats.
ISBN 978-0-7787-2230-4 (bound).--ISBN 978-0-7787-2238-0
(paperback).--ISBN 978-1-4271-1713-7 (html)

        1. Raccoon--Juvenile literature. 2. Raccoon--Infancy--
Juvenile literature. I. Title.

QL737.C26K345 2016   j599.76'32   C2015-908694-9
                                            C2015-908695-7

Library of Congress Cataloging-in-Publication Data

Names: Kalman, Bobbie, author.
Title: Raccoon family adventures / Bobbie Kalman.
Description: St. Catharines, Ontario ; New York, New York : Crabtree
  Publishing Company, [2016] | Series: Animal family adventures | Includes index.
Identifiers: LCCN 2016012275 (print) | LCCN 2016012798 (ebook) | ISBN
  9780778722304 (reinforced library binding : alk. paper) | ISBN
  9780778722380 (pbk. : alk. paper) | ISBN 9781427117137 (electronic HTML)
Subjects: LCSH: Raccoon--Behavior--Juvenile literature. | Raccoon--Juvenile
  literature.
Classification: LCC QL737.C26 K3435 2016 (print) | LCC QL737.C26 (ebook) |
  DDC 599.76/32--dc23
LC record available at http://lccn.loc.gov/2016012275

Crabtree Publishing Company

www.crabtreebooks.com   1-800-387-7650

Printed in Canada/052016/TL20160324

Published in Canada
Crabtree Publishing
616 Welland Ave.
St. Catharines, Ontario
L2M 5V6

Published in the United States
Crabtree Publishing
PMB 59051
350 Fifth Avenue, 59th Floor
New York, New York 10118

Published in the United Kingdom
Crabtree Publishing
Maritime House
Basin Road North, Hove
BN41 1WR

Published in Australia
Crabtree Publishing
3 Charles Street
Coburg North
VIC 3058

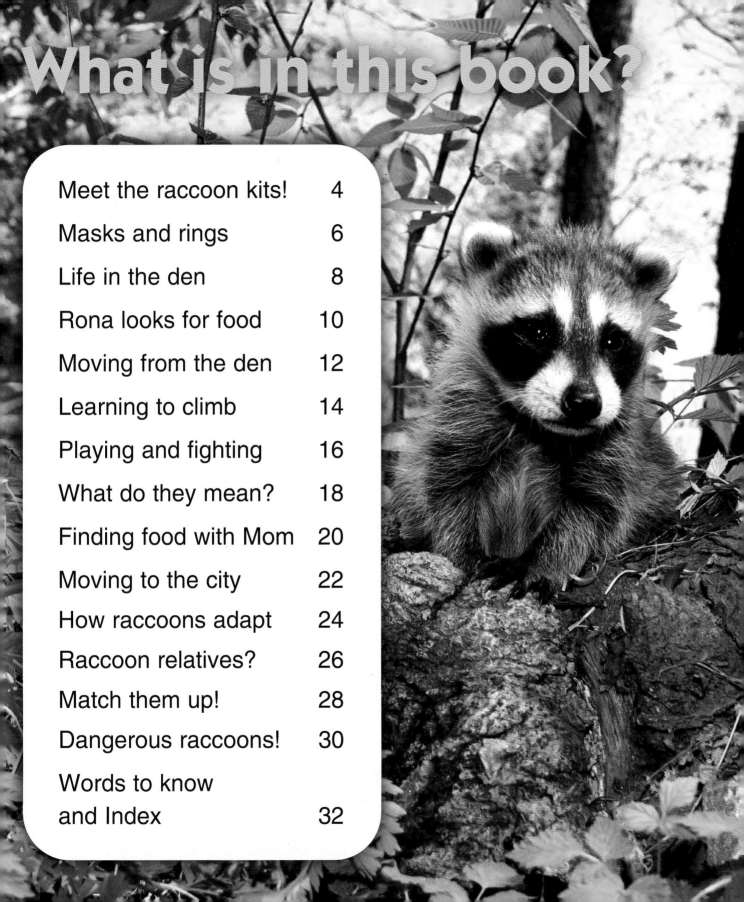

What is in this book?

Meet the raccoon kits!

Spring is here, and four raccoon kits were born in a **nursery den** high up in a tree. The kits, whom we shall call Ruby, Rosie, Ricky, and Ronny, need their mother, Rona.

Raccoons are animals called **mammals**. Mammal mothers **nurse**, or feed their babies milk from their bodies. The kits depend on Rona for milk, and they snuggle up to her to keep warm. Raccoon fathers do not help take care of the babies.

The kits are tiny and have a thin layer of fur. Their fur coats will grow thicker in a few weeks. Their eyes and ears are shut. They cannot hear or see, but they do make a lot of noise! When they cry, they sound like chirping birds.

Masks and rings

Like other raccoons, Ricky has dark markings over his eyes. He looks like he is wearing a mask! His mask started to show when he was a week old. His tail also has markings that look like rings.

Rosie and Ruby and
their brothers now look
different than when they
were born. Their ears
and eyes are open, their
noses are pointed, and
their fur is thicker.

Life in the den

The kits spend their first weeks sleeping and nursing in the den. To keep them safe, Rona does not allow the kits to leave the den, and she rarely leaves them alone.

8

The kits peek outside the hole in their den and see a strange new world, but they are not yet ready to explore it. Small animals like raccoon kits make easy meals for **predators** such as foxes and eagles. Predators hunt and eat other animals.

Rona looks for food

By the time the kits are a month old, they are more than twice the size they were when they were born. Rona will nurse them until they are two months old. Her milk is rich in fat and is all the kits need to grow. Rona leaves the den for only a few hours each evening to look for food. Like all raccoons, she is active at night. Raccoons can see well in the dark because their eyes have a special layer that reflects light. Their eyes seem to glow in the dark.

Raccoons are **omnivores**. They eat both plants and animals. Rona looks for frogs in a nearby stream and hunts a squirrel in the forest. There are also many plants she can eat. She is pulling one up by the roots. She won't be hungry for long!

Moving from the den

The kits are now six weeks old, and they are curious and want to go outside. They push each other out of the way to have a good look. Rosie climbs out and is holding on to Ruby so she will not fall. When Ruby goes back inside, Rosie hangs on to the edge of the den.

It is time for Rona to move the kits from the nursery den when they are two months old. She watches them climb down from the tree and carries them one at a time to one of her other dens. Her other dens may be between rocks, in hollow logs, or in holes in the ground. Ronny is peeking out of one of his new homes.

Learning to climb

Raccoons are excellent climbers. Ricky is hanging from a branch by his paws. His paws look like human hands with long fingers and short, curved claws. Raccoons are one of the few animals that can climb down head first. The kits had to climb down head first from their den in the tree trunk.

Besides trees, the kits also learn
to climb fences, walls, decks,
and rooftops. Ruby, Ricky,
and Ronny are high up in
a tree looking down at
Rosie, who is on her way
up to join them. Rona is
not far away. She makes
sure they are safe.

Playing and fighting

Raccoon kits love to play with their brothers and sisters. They run, climb, and explore their new den areas. One of the new dens is in a grassy area with many flowers. Rosie likes the bright colors of the flowers. She wonders if the flowers are good to eat.

Ruby peeks under a log to see what might be living there. Ricky and Ronny are playing hide-and-seek, but Ricky has no trouble finding Ronny. He is hiding in their new den. The kits also do a lot of play-fighting. Play-fighting helps them learn how to scare away predators that might want to eat them. Do you think Ronny and Rosie are scary, or are they just funny?

What do they mean?

Rona

Ronny and Ricky

Ruby

Rona and her kits **communicate** by making certain sounds. When they are hungry or scared, they hiss, bark, cry, growl, and scream. They snarl to scare away enemies and churr when they are happy. Churring sounds a lot like a cat purring. Raccoons also show what they want and how they feel by using **body language**, just as you do.

Rona growls, bears her teeth, and raises her paw to scare away an enemy. Ruby opens her mouth and cries to communicate that she needs help getting down from a tree. Ronny is hugging Ricky to show love. Rosie sticks out her tongue to keep cool when she is hot.

Rosie

Which children show that they care for each other the way Ronny and Ricky do? What sound and body language does Susan use to show how she feels? Which kit is sending the same message? Is Linda sticking out her tongue for the same reason that Rosie is? Why or why not? Liam is using the same body language as Rona, but is his message the same? Name five ways that you communicate using sounds and body language.

Susan

Liam

Linda

Atef and Badi

Finding food with Mom

Rona stopped nursing her kits when she moved them from the nursery den. She takes them out at night to look for food. The kits stay close to Rona so she can protect them from predators such as foxes and coyotes.

Every raccoon has a home range in which it can find enough food and water. The size of the home range depends on how much food is available. When there is plenty of food, raccoons stay in a small area. Rona makes sure her home range has trees and rivers or lakes. She and the kits can find water to drink and small animals, such as frogs, mice, and squirrels to eat there. They also eat acorns, berries, nuts, and birds' eggs.

Moving to the city

Part of Rona's home range is at the edge of a city. She showed the kits where they could find food there. The kits quickly learned that there is plenty of food in city parks, people's yards, and even in their homes. The kits are now much more **independent**, and in a few months, they will leave Rona to live on their own. Ricky and Ronny will live farther from their mother. Rosie and Ruby will stay closer to Rona's home range.

Ricky and Ronny now live in the city, where they can easily find food. They knock over trash cans and take food from bird feeders. They eat food that has been left out for pets and use parts of houses, such as chimneys, as their dens.

How raccoons adapt

Raccoons can live in many kinds of **habitats** because they are masters at **adapting**. To adapt means to change to suit a new way of life. Animals that adapt the best are those that eat almost any kind of food they find. Raccoons are not picky eaters! They even eat garbage—and they are not afraid to live near people.

Raccoons are smart animals that learn quickly. If they smell food, they can usually figure out how to get it. Their paws can grasp even small, thin objects. They are a lot like human hands. They help raccoons climb or open almost anything!

Rosie's palms can feel animals such as fish or frogs moving in water, so she can easily catch them. She also puts other food into water to soften it and feel it better. Raccoon paws are very sensitive when they are wet.

Raccoon relatives?

Raccoons belong to a small family of mammals called *Procyonidae*. Most mammals are covered in hair or fur, and their babies are born live. Mammal mothers feed their babies milk made in their bodies, just as Rona did. Four of the mammals on these pages are part of the *Procyonidae* family. Guess which ones are raccoon relatives!

Coatis live in Central and South America. They are great climbers. How is this coati like a raccoon?

The red panda lives in Asia. It has a face mask and tail rings. Is it related to raccoons?

Raccoon dogs live in forests in Europe and Asia. They have thick fur and eat small animals. Are they dogs or raccoons?

Kinkajous have short fur and small ears. They live in forests in Central and South America.

The crab-eating raccoon has short fur. It lives in South America.

Ringtails live in Mexico and in southwestern United States.

Answers

Coatis, kinkajous, ringtails, and crab-eating raccoons are raccoon relatives. Red pandas and raccoon dogs are not part of the Procyonidae family.

Match them up!

The pictures on these pages will help you remember what you have learned about raccoons. Match the pictures to the information in the box on the next page.

A

B

C

Match the pictures with this information.

1. Raccoons put their food in water to soften it and feel it.
2. Raccoons are excellent climbers. They can climb up and down trees, even when they are very young.
3. Raccoon kits are born in a nursery den and stay there for about two months.
4. Raccoons are active at night. Their eyes have a special layer that helps them see in the dark.
5. Coyotes are raccoon predators.
6. Raccoons can live where people live.

Answers

1. E, 2. C, 3. A, 4. F, 5. B, 6. D

Dangerous raccoons!

Raccoons seem very cute, but they can be very dangerous to pets and people. Adult raccoons can kill a dog by biting or clawing it. They can also pass fleas, ticks, and some harmful diseases, such as **rabies**, to both other animals and people. Their **feces**, or poop, may contain **roundworms**, which can be very harmful to humans. Never touch raccoon droppings, and never go near a raccoon! Be sure to warn your friends about how dangerous raccoons can be!

Do not leave pet food where raccoons can get it. Raccoons will keep coming back and could make you and your pets very sick.

What to do!

These are some helpful tips to keep raccoons away:

- Make sure your garbage cans have lids that are tightly closed.
- Pick up any fallen fruit.
- Ask your parents to call a wildlife removal company for help.

Get rid of pet doors at your home!

Words to know

Note: Some boldfaced words are defined where they appear in the book.

bacteria (bak-TEER-ee-uh) noun
Very tiny living things made of single cells

body language (BOD-ee LANG-gwij) noun
Communication using gestures, posture, or facial expressions

communicate (kuh-MYOO-ni-keyt) verb
To exchange feelings and thoughts through sounds, smells, or body language

habitat (HAB-i-tat) noun The natural place where a plant or animal lives

independent (in-di-PEN-duh-nt) adjective
Able to act and live without help from others

mammal (MAM-uh-l) noun A warm-blooded animal that is covered in hair or fur and gives birth to live young

nursery den (NUR-suh-ree den) noun
A shelter used by animals, in which they give birth to babies and care for them

omnivore (OM-nuh-vawr) noun An animal that eats both plants and other animals

predator (PRED-uh-ter) noun An animal that hunts and eats other animals

roundworm (ROUND-wurm) noun
A small worm that lives in the intestines of mammals and can cause serious illness

A noun is a person, place, or thing. A verb is an action word that tells you what someone or something does. An adjective is a word that tells you what something is like.

Index